#creative devotion

Original artwork and poetry by
Hatt Kelley

FIRST EDITION, MAY 2017
Copyright © 2017 by Practice Kindness Publications

Published in the United States by Practice Kindness Publications.

The Library of Congress has cataloged this edition as follows:
Kelley, Harriett "Hatt" 1957, 12/3 -
Creative Devotion /by Hatt Kelley – 1st U.S. ed.

ISBN: 978-1544864549

Printed in the United States of America

Book cover and interior design by Doreen Hann
Cathryn Castle Garcia, editor
cathryncastle.com

Acknowledgments

I belong to the Blanche Dubois school of Life. I am dependent on the kindness of strangers, lovers, and friends for most things—including this book. If Leigh Medeiros had not hosted #creativedevotion on Facebook, I might not have written 96 poems. If Chris Zydel did not teach Painting from the Wild Heart, I might not have started painting every day. If Cathryn Castle Garcia had not approached me with the idea of publishing a book of the poetry, you wouldn't have it in your hands now. If Doreen Hann had not formatted the book as beautifully as she has, it would not be as pleasing to the eye.

And the gratitude goes further back. If I did not learn to love and live more fully from the patients and their families that I served as a chaplain, then I would lack words and concepts found in the poetry. If I did not have mentors and colleagues and teachers, then I would not have worked as a chaplain. If I had not been a hairstylist in San Francisco during the beginning of the AIDS pandemic and witnessed the suffering of so many, I would have never studied meditation and energy healing. If I had not healed myself, I would probably not be here, or if I lived, it would be in a much darker place.

If I had not been born into a loving dysfunctional family that fostered an interactive heart and an independent brain, would I have moved to San Francisco? Would I have loved and married and created family here? And how would I be free to create if it were not for the love and support of my husband, children, granddaughter, siblings, nieces, nephews, chosen family, and friends—in person, or not yet met?

I dedicate this book to all of you, with a deep bow of love and appreciation.

Thank you.

Hall Kelly

Hatt's beautiful book is a testament to the alignment that happens when we devote ourselves to creativity, when we show up every day regardless of insecurities, fear, restlessness, or lack of preconceived notion about the work. It's a testament to the portal that opens when we have faith – if not in ourselves, then in the act of creation.

In devotion we come to understand that creativity always joins us at that pre-arranged meeting spot, that our fear is always replaced with flow (or at least tempered by it), and that we are as much a witness to the creation as we are the makers of it.

I believe Hatt's words yearned to be born as poems, that color and form ached to merge and be expressed as her paintings. Her immense devotion is what allowed them to come through and be shared with us.

Hatt exalts in capital 'L' Life - not just the easy, lovely bits, but the hard, messy, painful stuff too. Her book is filled with prayers, both reverent and irreverent, that seem to cast a line from earthly observation to spiritual truth.

The imagery in Hatt's poems is not only the imagery of our cultural landscape, but also the imagery of one's inner landscape too. She enables us to see emotion and thought made manifest. Her abstract paintings don't so much illustrate the words, as they serve to illuminate them. Unsurprisingly, so many of them recall the aesthetic of stained glass windows. There is a holy wondering and a sacred witnessing here. Light emanates from both word and image.

I know every human that collaborates with creativity and expresses their truth, as Hatt has done here, helps make the world a bit more whole, for art heals both artist and witness.

We need more poems. We need more paintings. We need more creative devotion. We need more people like Hatt.

~ Leigh Medeiros, 2017

Why creative devotion?

As a chaplain and energy minister, I have sat with thousands of people who were either facing life threatening illness or dying from one. As you could imagine, my heart was broken regularly. But I noticed that by listening to people's stories, my heart was breaking open and I was learning to love more deeply. There were shared truths in the stories; yearning for missed opportunities, longing for greater intimacy with loved ones, the fading fantasy of "tomorrow." There were surprises too; the lovely benefit of slowing down even when it was tinged with loss. The profound joy of sitting in the warmth of the sun, or in eating a few bites of a cheese burrito, or in holding a stranger's hand.

One of the prices I paid for all this wisdom was a slowly increasing grief load. Even though I cried daily as a part of my self-care, I knew a time would come when I would need to put down the load. I am so grateful that I recognized the time and retired before burning out or barricading myself from my emotions. It took several years of spiritual practices to mourn it all.

Slowly, I felt my "bubbling aliveness" returning; and with it came joy and generative creativity. It was as if I was given a fresh chance to slip into the flow of life. I admit, at first I resisted. I felt some survivor guilt at being given the chance to have fun and create when so many I had grown to love had not. And I felt a bit rusty and resistant to opening fully to the flow. It meant I had to change. My joke was that I loved change—it was transitions I hated! But truly, I had to shift my sense of identity, again. The same Spring energy that helps a weed burst through a crack in the sidewalk, was making it very difficult for me to stay my same sad self.

When I read an invitation to create something every day and post it on Facebook for the next 48 days, I jumped at the chance. #creativedevotion was the brainchild of Leigh Medeiros, a Facebook friend I have never met, but whom I love and to whom I will forever be grateful. For the next 48 days, I sat in the morning, opened my heart and mind, and let a poem come to me. I kept waiting for it to get hard, but the opposite happened. When I said, "Yes," joy, ease, and creative energy flowed in. I did a second cycle of 48 days writing poetry and this book was born.

Next, I felt called to attend "Wild Hearted Painting" with Chris Zydel. It was as if my creative inhibitions had died. Now, it is challenging for me to not create every day. I am pulled into the flow and have gotten giddy with it. My hopes for you, dear reader, is that you are inspired by my offerings to create whatever you are called to do. This is a very selfish desire. We need you. We need you to show up, create, and join the dance. I remember a friend, dear to my heart, making a distinction between simple and easy. Devoting yourself to creativity is simple; devote some time, energy and focus every day to creating something with heart and intention. But devoting yourself to creativity may not be easy. You, too, may confront some resistance; maybe in the form of perfectionism, or needing to renew your identity, or in engaging your emotions. But, my friend, where there is life there is possibility.

I love adventure stories! Please connect with me on Facebook at Hatt Kelley's Creative Conspiracy.

My original artwork is available for purchase at hattkelley.com.

Blessings on your Journey!

Table of Contents

#creativedevotion

Cycle One

We spoke of stemware.

How silly with such little time,
I'll miss so much, though I know
I go to live with God, and will stay
as close as Nana's cheek when she
bent down to kiss the boo-boo.
Still, I'll miss the talks where women
share the struggle of authoring their lives;
while meeting the needs of others.
My girls will be alone with love,
loss, and no chance to ask for that recipe.
No chance to be at Grammy's house,
with warm sweet smells,
where soft laughter greets the old stories
and raised voices shout good bye as the party dwindles.
When words failed, we spoke of love in code.
We spoke of the good china and how to store it safe.

The Present Moment

How curious to be
bogged down by life's
necessity.
When with a twist of kaleidoscope,
buoyant love colors eternity
caught in this very moment.
Angels and Saints wait
with patient glee
for all of us to see
the light of heaven here.

.

Dancing through Space

You and Earth are dancing through Space together.
Pay attention to the Music. Try not to trample on her feet.

Unseen Allies

We greeted you when you arrived,
small spark of great divinity.
We helped to keep your spark alive,
gentle breath fanning ember.
We witnessed when you cried,
mouth choked with ash
as small dreams died aborning.
If we could soothe your malcontent
we'd consider it time well spent
but it would defeat the purpose.
For here you came to feed your flame
and burn out impurities that stain
the canvas which contains
your masterpiece.
We watch and love you from afar
but close enough to catch the stars
which glisten in your tears.
If you could only hear our song
the one we sing through out your days
in praise of all you have created-
If you could see how this glorious mess
supports expanding gracefulness-
Would you still strive? Or
would you relax and abide with us
side by side with the eternal flame?

Thanks for Sharing

Sometimes, when I've been brave

and spoke my heart,

my knees tremble, not with fear

for I have gauged well my words and audience,

but with the effort to remain upright

under the weight of Grace.

The Passion.

Do you know why
God did not make
Jesus a woman?
No one would
have noticed
her sacrifice.

Later years

World weary flesh
shaped by time and stress
lays heavy on her shoulders
like daddy's overcoat
in a game of dress up.
Sorrows curve the spine
casting eyes down
till blue skies seem made up,
a bedtime story
to entertain the child
who covers her eyes to hide.
Buoyant life abounds
just beyond body
and angels pause
to share the wait
and lift the burden
of her long story.
Trust, like Love,
Frees the mind.
Ageless light
lifts the blinds
for those who
choose to see.
Eventually, you slip
the cloak and bare
shouldered Grace
enfolds self into
Self, embraced.

Liminality

Within a sea of possibility
no mirror or eyes reflect
back to me the borders
of my identity.
Yet there is a witness
to the dance in the ocean
of energy, a play of light
flashes musically
its notes linger.
I am the great I am,
but in my smallness too
I create a universe within
a multiverse and love
lasts the longest.

For Love or Fear

The energy behind
everything
is love or fear.
Fear constricts,
Love expands.
What I hear
is up to me.
I choose to see
you expressing
love, or if not love,
asking for my help
to get there.

Through the Glass Darkly

If you are blessed to be
instructed by a toddler
take it as a chance to see
how much are we hardwired.
Nature/nurture, tinker/tailor
all in future time, before
choices dig the trench.
Free will leads the way
before we're tempered by
rods or treats, to join the game
our families play on larger teams–
concentric circles evermore.
Taught the rules and steps
to take, or gestures which dictate
our place, bogged down by
runners in the race,
until the inner voice
sounds like someone else entirely.
Take a chance
observe the child
resist the urge to teach;
listen hard, relearn to see
the freedom just to be.

The Streetcar

Unsteady on your feet,
you crawled over to take the seat
right next to mine.
Head down you didn't see
disdainful glances
instead you whispered to me
parts of your story.
How being on the streets was like
teetering backward on canyon edge
heels dangling, arms windmilling
no one to catch or break your fall.
But things were slightly better now
new glasses from that homeless team
you told me of an angel
like from a dream
you were pretty sure was real.

Tracking life around

The cityscape, with time, becomes
a multileveled land.
Where stories float
like shackled ghosts
tethered in place
by the memories of passersby.
Here Mary dodged
some falling glass.
There Joey declared
his love for John,
and claimed his new ID.
This is the doorway
where Deb slept, and wept,
and dreamed a different life.
Where people live, debris is left,
glittering on the ground.
Be careful where you step
downtown, if you fear
tracking life around.

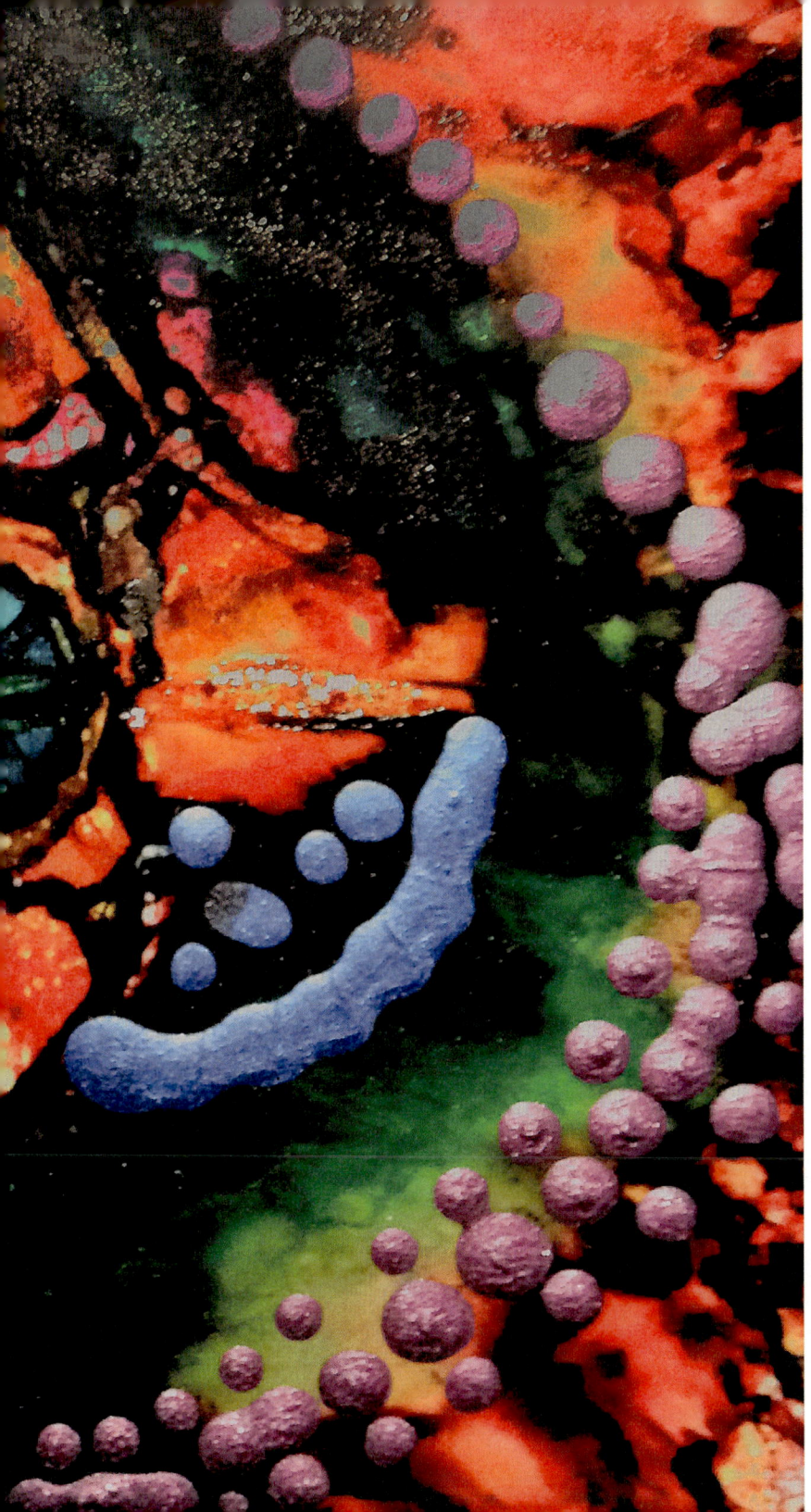

Missed Communication

She said that she was blessed,
Jesus was good and close
no matter what, she'd be alright.
She worried about the doctor though,
so sweet a young man.
He repeated carefully
the prognosis, certain that
she misunderstood, or was in shock.
She complimented the job
he did and tried to share her faith.
She understood the end was near,
but in truth, it held no fear.
For Life was just beginning.

Thirty years Married

Our love a foundation
from which we both
branch out into the world
bearing fruit for ourselves
and others to enjoy.
Juices, not sticky sweet,
but rich, warm succulence
that dribbles off our chins
and down our throats
to feed our hearts.
A sacrament, two lives
entwined, like vines
deeply rooted, clinging
to each other breathing
in the soft blue air
of twilight.

The Getaway

Just a half hour away
by car, a change of scene,
brings fresh vision to witness
a love so familiar, so close.
As close as the back of my knee,
you know how easy that is to see?
Exactly, but, there's a new trail and
us, an old pair, strolling with hands
shading eyes against the glare.
"Look at the view," murmuring
to each other, "life is good."
And so it is, with you.
Back home our lives in little piles,
reminders of what needs doing,
but here? We're stripped down
to the essentials, the water, the sun
and love.

Sleep Walking

There is a walkway in Chicago,
with flashing neon lights,
meant to distract the weary
folks on connecting flights.
A disembodied voice instructs
you keep moving on
instead of tripping, or God forbid,
slowing down fellow travelers.
"Keep walking," drones in your ear,
speed is the highest value,
like running in place
you leave no trace of you
passing through.
Somehow this is the whole
manmade world to me,
frenetic lights and sounds
demanding movement which
for all the world
I hear as "Sleep Walking."

Your passing

When you left
I lost my words
as if your passing
passed on your reserve.
Not your peace,
for in truth, you never
had much of that in life.
Nor passivity since it's
been lively enough,
not jumping joy
but no dirge either.
Images delight eye
stilled in my mind,
the longing to share
remains as strong,
but action speaks
louder. Love cries
from the rooftops.
Your spot reserved
the empty chair noted.
Slowly words surface
to be served at the table
for family, and other guests.

The Missing

How can we see what's missing?
With negative space
what's not there helps define what is
What about the bigger picture?
How do we find
the missing "who,"
the uninvited?
No place set at the table,
no empty chair to show
that someone isn't there.
No search party
seek the ones
not gathered in.
They sit outside
the circle of warmth
watching from the shadows.

Insomnia

First, there is the body
demanding attention
itchy nose, cold feet
full bladder calls
stumble to the pot
don't look at the clock
lights too bright
don't think of the hour.
Don't think!
Mind clicks in
thoughts "what if"
"if only" triggers shouldna,
and her sisters, couldna
and oughtna. Feelings
rise–dripping details
that tomorrow will
resolve themselves
but now serve to sever
peaceful slumber.
Dreams derailed
by a system
too sensitive to sleep.
Ask the angels
to wrap round their wings
and muffle your weary soul
rest deep just not for long.

Platitudes

There are times when words
must convey more
than they can carry.
When grief and fear
thicken the air between
those who've lost
and we who watch close by.
Grief's a nasty neighborhood
occupied by future ghosts
who haunt mind, if not heart
with horrific visions.
Guilty with the thought
"Thank God, it isn't me!"
With phantom blinded eye
we see your grief etched face,
and sense a sliver of
excruciating separation.
My heart wants nothing
more than to flee
even the possibility
of joining in your suffering.
Without meeting your
shattered gaze, my hand
lands clumsy on yours,
as I say, "I'm sorry for your loss."

Life in the Margins

Marginalia, sounds sexy right?
Those illuminated manuscripts
that used to be in churches
but now live in museums
copied by a monk
in the Middle Ages
doing his 9 to 5 in a
silent library.
When he got bored
or perhaps inspired
he'd do a little sketch
Brother John sleeping
his mouth wide open,
or a ditty about
dust motes dancing
in the slanting sun,
right there next to scripture.
An academic granted
the monastic scribbles
their slightly sexy title.
In Modern times like these
when we all take turns
living in the margins,
outside the gospel
according to authorities,
I wonder who will note us where?

The two Trees

There are two trees
"Knowledge," should
have a different name,
like "compare and condemn."
Myth ties its limbs,
an esplanade of Sorrow.
Serpent, eternal She,
temptation, fall,
it's soil fear and shame,
drops poisoned fruit
to call busy bees,
spreading it's pollen
under a bitter sun.
The other is "Life,"
no bondage here,
just boundless possibility
a cacophony of choice.
Where do you land?

Is the Sun out Today?

"It's been so long
since I saw the sun."
She looked away
toward the window,
from the hospital bed.
It isn't the weather
she's talking about.
That golden Light
whose warmth
penetrates deeply
bringing relaxation
and the first deep breath
she's drawn in a month.
She faces the window
and speaks in code,
her hand stretched
out toward me,
about Hope.

To the Priest who said No

You said that girls couldn't serve.
It's training for priestly duty,
never mind that there have been
girls on the altar for fifty years.
We must protect the institution
from those little powerhouses
in pigtails. It's over 2000 years old!
Even gold threads in altar cloths
(stitched by woman's hands)
can tarnish in the dust of ages.
Too risky to throw open doors
to fresh faced kids, who do they
think they are anyway, God?

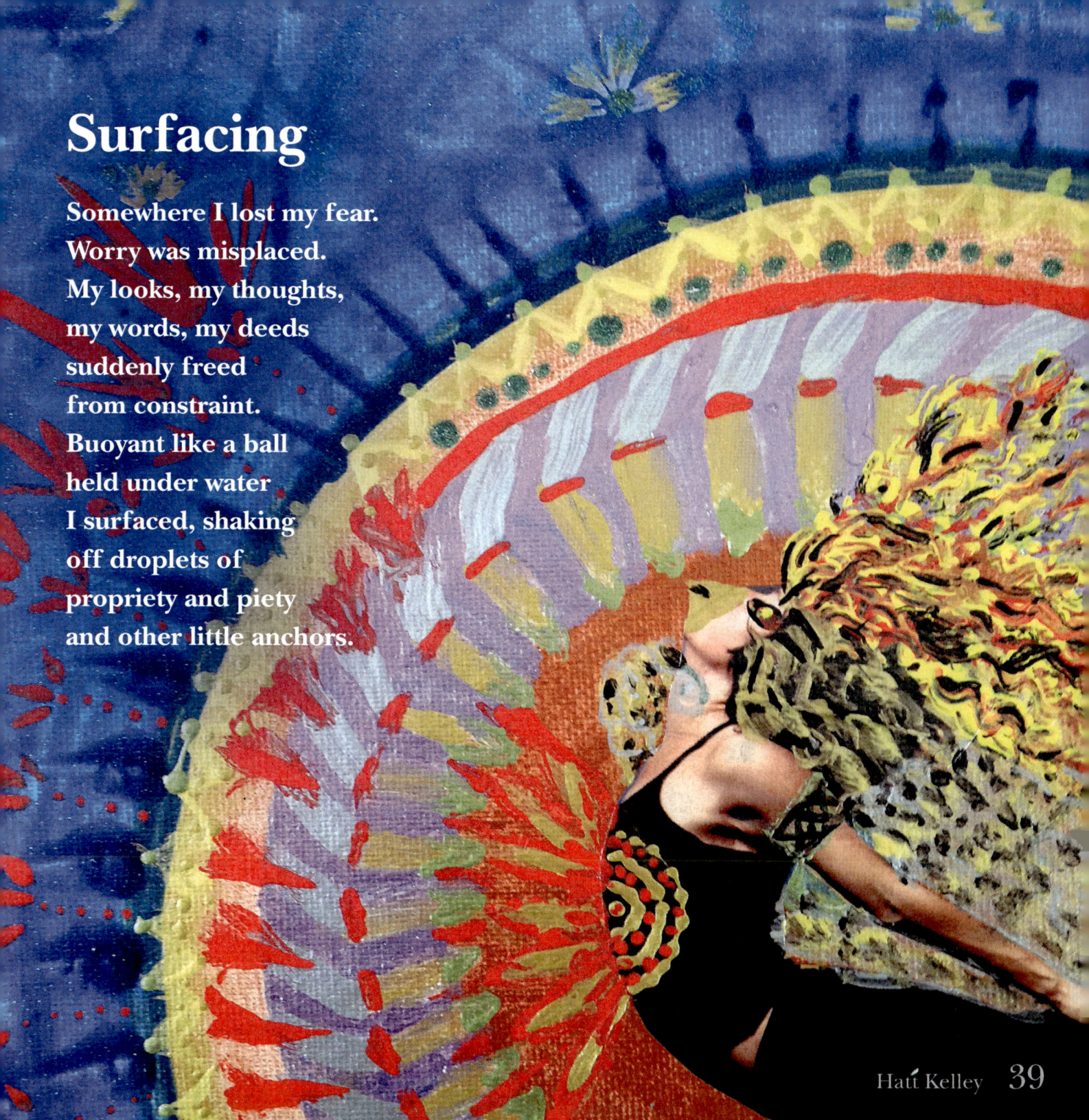

Surfacing

Somewhere I lost my fear.
Worry was misplaced.
My looks, my thoughts,
my words, my deeds
suddenly freed
from constraint.
Buoyant like a ball
held under water
I surfaced, shaking
off droplets of
propriety and piety
and other little anchors.

Should be Seen not Heard

Sometimes you needn't
raise your voice
or even speak one word
just being seen
for where you've been
can cause a scene.
For some
causing a scene
is righteous,
like throwing a lifeline
to a drowning man,
risking your safety
from the shore.
But some of us
are treading dangerous water
and if we cause a scene
we might be seen
going down
for the third time.

Is helping a trap?

I don't mean working
in community,
where the same ole gang
stays late to clean up,
or comes early to set up,
usually both.
That's sharing the load.
Bless those helpers!
No, I'm talking
hierarchical helping.
Not sharing because
a relationship is required for that.
Barry's sitting in the store front,
drinking his daily cup of Peet's
his friend always brings,
when a guy going by
drops a quarter into it.
We laughed when Barry told the story,
shaking his head.
He said he thanked the guy,
and drank the coffee anyway.
After all it was Peet's!
And the guy meant well.

Please don't call me good.

There are certain words
that I don't get, like "nice."
Too subjective!
What's it mean?
Call me kind, or loving,
I'm down with that.
"Interesting" is another.
I use it to take a breather,
like when I'm opening a gift
and don't know what it is,
or when considering a
character defect that I
want to change, but am
unsure how it will unfold.
Words can be tricky,
bland as beige or
flashing gold like fish
right beneath the surface
before darting away.

Intersecting Stories

Where do you step
into the stream
of someone else's story?
The hidden one that serves
as source for all
that flows downstream.
Once upon a time
the little girl was shushed
too much
And the little hero boy
slayed imaginary foes,
saved the castle, and won
the soothing love he sought.
Her voice too loud and words too blunt
as she bursts her hidden damn.
He wields authority like sword,
a bully on an internal quest.
Without a guide rope or a tow
wade lightly in their shallows
lay stones to show your path
or drain your swamp as a final edit
Our lives and stories intersect,
like river joining sea
the strongest tide turns the tale
that's told of you and me.

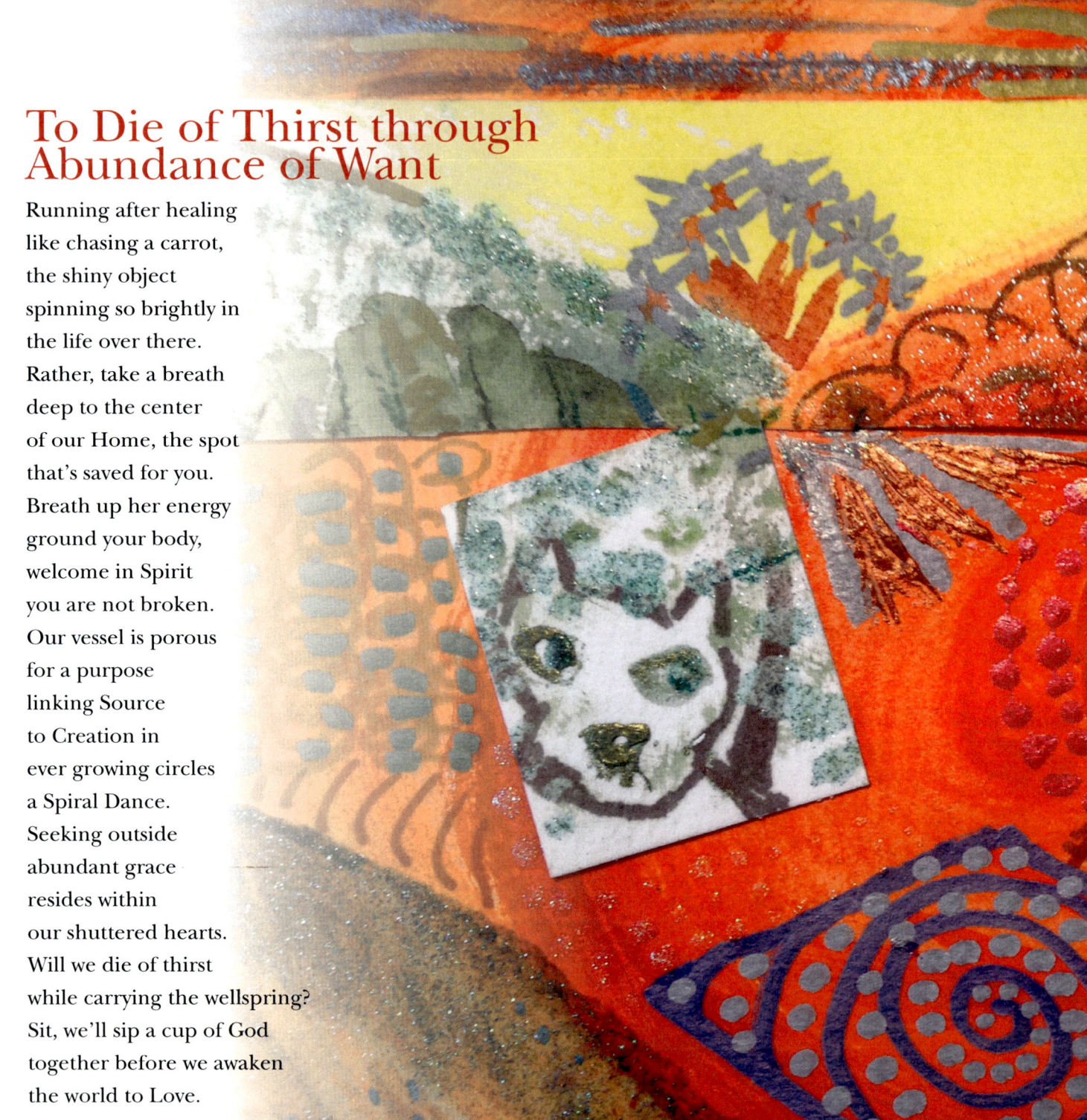

To Die of Thirst through Abundance of Want

Running after healing
like chasing a carrot,
the shiny object
spinning so brightly in
the life over there.
Rather, take a breath
deep to the center
of our Home, the spot
that's saved for you.
Breath up her energy
ground your body,
welcome in Spirit
you are not broken.
Our vessel is porous
for a purpose
linking Source
to Creation in
ever growing circles
a Spiral Dance.
Seeking outside
abundant grace
resides within
our shuttered hearts.
Will we die of thirst
while carrying the wellspring?
Sit, we'll sip a cup of God
together before we awaken
the world to Love.

Gather In

Come, come, awaken
from your dream
wild and wonderful
or nightmare. Come.
Gather close where ever
you are, here is welcome.
Come. Who are you called?
Stranger, Wanderer, Mystic,
share story, break your fast,
leave loneliness. Take a sip.
Come, you are free to come
and go, please join the circle.
There is room, stretch out.
Be seen, and see how gently
you are held, sit near the fire.
Warm your hands, Come
hear the song, lay down
your weary bones,
and rest a while
until sleep descends again.

On the Way Home

I stand transfixed on my walk home
to see the wheeling grace in flight
two red tails and two ravens
dance their battle in fading light.
I think of symbolic meanings
Spirit Messenger and Sacred Law
dueling above my domain and
wonder what the signs predict.
Laughing at myself,
the center of the world
I glimpse with eagle eye
the biped far below.
Being calls to Being
reverberating Light
God laughs in Joy
amused by the perspectives.

Dressing for the Dance

Wardrobe has always
been for me less fashion
and more identity.
Like Clark Kent needing
glasses, not a cape.
Armor not to protect
from eye of the beholder,
instead magic to project
in shades bolder, the "I am"
needed for today's (ad)venture.
As years and habit
shape my form
the window dressing
import lessens.
For having lived so many roles,
my closet's full of choices
form follows function
as long as I can move
I might as well dance.

Communion
with a Tree

Watch winds bounce
leaves on branches high
interweaving dance
an entire stand in sway.
Mesmerizing motions
raise spirit up
from weary stillness,
soaring on sightlines
free and then stunned
to be still bound by body.
Imagine now connection switch
from Tree down to humanity.
Rooted tall, standing placed
amongst the elders whose
deaths have given way
to Life, sustaining centuries.
Green gift to others here
clears the air, sharing shade.
Still on our watch, ages fly
sunrise blurring blessed dark
layering rings to bark.
What's that among our roots?

Today's Offering

Have you ever been brave?
Mind said walk, but
heart said stay
Fear choked you
in your tracks but
heart said turn and
so slowly ever so
your turning turned the tide.
Maybe you failed magnificently,
fear and fortitude glowing,
face front to censure,
the obstacle too big to budge.
Maybe I haven't but
I saw it today.
And my heart burst
my mind wide open.

Staggered Writing

Free my words
from their incidental
birthplace and
see them stumble

to the sacred
stand expanded.
Fear roots snares
on worn page and words
flail about trying to create.
Embodied vision
steadies gait
tempering instinct
but lacking faith.
Intuition steps lightly
around stillborn originality
passion plays instrumental
yet practical wisdom
dictates the dance.

A test of Faith

Can we hold each other
gently, gently in cupped
hands like water lifted
to quench thirst.
Can we open to each other
and share story
unfolding before us
open not editing.
Can we see each other
look, look a spark
is here glowing
ember of divinity.
Can we be together
distinct yet bonded
freely committed
to being not doing.
Come, we can stay
in healing presence
nestled in soft silver light.
No hope is false.

First Do No Harm

Hip to this oath
though not a doc
I can heal myself at least.
And who's to say
who may see me
on my way to wearing
a mantle of Grace?
And having seen for herself
could welcome in
transcendence for a cuppa
settling in for a chat
open up to what may be
a lovely rest
head snuggled
in the lap of God?

Community Life

Like a rock tumbled
by the flow of a river
polishes the stone,
being authentically me
in relationship to community
knocks off the rough edges
of small sins and
shallow indulgences.
Unwilling to leave,
nor to submerge,
I surrender. Not my
POV for that would be
a form of flight,
rather I give up the fight
to change yours
and by holding ground
we make it holy.
By showing up again, again
with aching need and unruly gifts
the quiet clashes wear smooth our souls
like river rocks or prayer beads.

You are not alone

Restless heart
bleeding darkness
you are not alone.
Circling the depths
you are surrounded
by burning pillars of light
loving your struggle.
Tend your fire,
cup hands around
trembling flame,
you belong here.
We need you.
When rejection weighs
weary on your head
remember that
fierce love has your back.
You are needed now.
Do not match
the haters' fear.
Do not hoard Life
like a dragon sleeping
atop his gold.
Let light out, a beacon,
we will find you.
Commingled light
compounded fire
will cleanse the World.

A saint's day (robbing Rumi)

Witness your heart pumping love every second of every minute of every hour of day in day out. Gratitude forever floods astral body. Love is seeping in even as it flows out to others. When were we taught to deny it's inward flow? Time worn scar tissue create blockages and stems circulation. Beauty, withered dry dies adorning empty desert. Fire, wind, water, sculpts rocky landscape. Lovelovelove pumps relentless grace wearing away fear, dissolving shame bares the glittering bones of possibility. Breathe deeply in, "Life is no caravan filled with despair come, yet again, come."

Kiss it up to God

A saying for kids
like the five-second rule
with spiritual pretensions
dropped goodies were kissed up
offered to God for cleansing
then gobbled with gusto
I am no longer a child
my offerings not fallen fruit
with layers of polite repression
I kiss up creativity unfettered
words seeking to convey
beliefs replete with bawdiness
Bite into frivolous phrases
spit out presumed causality
suck joy, the marrow of memories,
lick sorrows' drippings from my fingers
Does my crudeness frighten you?
God laughs through me.

Your loss put me at Sea

Grief a miasma
blocks the sun.
Daily soundings,
sometimes hourly,
marks the depths
of grief and longing.
Days to years
small routines of
ship bound life
stay the course.
When Joy is sighted
from the nest
remembered sorrow,
the moment of loss,
is guilt caressed
like those metal balls
rolled in the captain's hands
obsessively.
Will I choose to climb
from the cross?
claim resurrection
cut my badge of trauma
worn with perverse pride
drop the duffle of heavy emptiness
and turn towards home?
Light thrown in darkness
shows the way.
Courage, so like love,
may anchor me in port.

Capitalism

Buy stuff,
fill the void
it's patriotic!
Forget about
the third world
and the planet.
We deserve it
or we wouldn't
have it, right?
Buy the right
stuff and you'll
be in the golden
circle, don't worry
about the golden calf.

Bon Voyage

How do you
handle tripping?
Do you jump up
looking to see
who's watching?
Do you curse
cracked sidewalk
or stubbed toe?
Do you hate
on yourself
or does fear catch
your breath, as arms
windmill wildly.
How you do one
is how you do all
Can you love the trip?

Whispered Offering

If only my words
could comfort
like every hug
ever ached for
and received
combined and refined
to an elixir of belonging
of being witnessed
and welcomed in
certain that the depths
of loneliness had
lost their dark pull
in the face of acceptance
from companions
on the walk home
If my words had that power
fear might make me stammer
but still they'd be
a whispered offering
from my heart to yours

In the Now

Awaken and rise
rub the grit
from your eyes
stretch your limbs.
Here is Beauty
in this very moment
right now, right now.
Sleep is wonderful
eventful rest
realigning internal
garden, but here
healing is ripe fruit
bite in and feel
the juices run,
pure insight,
to refresh barren
homelands.
Gently float above
the old story told
again, again, again
to self and all
around the dying fire.
Joy awaits you
on the threshold.
Come! Outside
the cherished wounds
and burnished lies,
new life is waiting
to hear new music
step into the dance.

The Long Goodbye

Some say we begin to die
the moment of our birth.
If that is true
then the words
I've shared with you
began to dwindle
as they're formed
flowing into mind
onto keys out to you
gentle readers.
I have no proof to
disavow that view
but my vision
is longer–we're born
yes and die yes

but death is
yet another birth
where arms of light enfold
Again, again, again
When should
the long goodbye
begin? My words
will fade quicker
than old ink brown
on paper turned gold
with age a digitized
turn of phrase misplaced in
transit post on post.
But no thing is lost in Love.
That's what I been saying.

#creativedevotion

Cycle Two

Were you told to be smaller?

When you were young and small
trying to grow up and be strong
did they say you were wrong?
Wrong shape, wrong sound,
wrong thoughts, not fit
to be seen, much less
to express yourself.
They made it you,
but it was they
who couldn't
be the way
they were.
So you
tried
to
fit in.
No way
to be what
they said, just
to be tolerated.
You needed love
instead and there was
no room to breathe much
less be the magnificent you
that heaven sent to be here in
the world. You stayed incognito
to be safe, but now the time to be
as big, as big, as you can be has come.
All the world is waiting to love you now.
For our sake, come out, come out and be
the only you that you can be and stop passing
on judgment to the next kid. It's healing time now.

Oh Tender Spirit

Oh Tender Spirit,
Not green with envy
but with new growth,
do not trample your
sweet innocence
because you fear fear.
There is guidance hidden
here in the quickened
breath. Breathe deeply
and see; the next step
beckons you forward.
Be cautious, carry yourself
like a glass that's over full
with magic, but keep moving
in the dance.
Fear is only one of many
colors on the wheel,
and though it may not
always be safe out
in the world, to freeze
is to die prematurely.
Or worse,
to choose to trade
your precious gift
to simply exist
in a fog of lost joys,
may be the only sin.
Choose Life.
Listen to the music within.

Addiction

Why desire to escape your life?
I understand the need to leave
the aching body or
ease the racing mind
just for a moment—the time
it takes to deeply draw a breath.
The need to be cocooned
in calm, like a kid hiding
under the covers, shutting
out the chaos of other people's
wants and your demands.
Yes, I get that need, but
how then does that sorry
peace, based on externals
a puff of smoke, the magic cup,
become so vital to identity?
A constant calling, so hard
to ignore, that it swallows
you whole, and then feasts upon
your children's children left
wandering in the shadows.
Is there a villain in the story?
And if the blame is cast
does it stop the longing,
the sorry longing, to be
any where but here
and any one but me?

Wait!
What was
I doing?

Have you ever lost your words,
just drawn a blank midsentence,
or walked into another room
and wondered why you're there?
What if that moment was not
a glitch in your mental firing
but a detour in awareness,
encapsulated enlightenment.
A brief glimpse of eternity,
might well divert attention.
Struck still, you stand
and try to see the prior
moment's focus,
not meant to be,
now all's strangely new.
There you are, ancient star,
standing in your socks,
majestic wisdom and
awakened heart,
scratching your head
just trying to be OK.

What's your game?

Life's a pinball machine
birthday bumping birthday
ricocheting along worn routes
garish lights and raucous songs.
Even the allusion is archaic,
do arcades exist today
in our digital society?
We walk with screens
before our eyes,
playing words with friends
we've never met,
or worse, we vent our hate
and venom with no connection
except the wireless.
And yet, I love my peeps
whose hearts I've met

via their writing on the internet.
Still, I worry that I may miss
some opportunity for bliss
distracted as I am; and then
there's those who wander by
and those who may be sitting out
the current game we play.
What wisdom may be lost
or future genius tossed aside
because they can't abide
surfing the latest tide or fashion.
When will I reach the end
of my willingness to teach
myself the most recent trend?
Are we the ball, or the machine,
and if my spinning ball
is swallowed by the gaping maw
of the machine, where will I be
when I run out of free games?

Ghosts in the Castro

I saw you on my way home
in the fading light.
My breath caught till
I realized it wasn't you
in the gathering blue.
Perhaps a genetic match;
a small man leans against the wall.
His hands cupping the flare
of flame as glowing ember catches.
I long to hug him as dark gathers,
would he throw his head back
and laugh if I acted the fool?
I love him now,
for you were resurrected
gently there for a moment.
You are always with me.
Gentle Spirit filled with pride
for who I have become.
I am grateful to be so cherished.
But, last evening, on my way home,
You came back wholly,
and I was whole and free,
right before night fell.

Today's Sermon

Why is it easier to believe
in a vengeful angry God
than one who has Mercy?
Is it longing to have
our defects seen and sorted
like cleaning beans, picked over?
A way to know we matter.
Perhaps we seek to ease the shame
by trying to be perfect,
graven image lacking life,
impossibly consistent dream.
Or if our God condemns and hates,
then we too can blame, and
indulge in casting fate,
instead of stones.
How much harder it is to be
a flame of Love and Charity.
To forgive, again, again, again,
myself and others too
our tiny wants and greedy needs
for being a human who grieves
and far too often falls.
If we believed that we are loved
no matter what was going on
we might resist making a list
of all our faults, and recognize
instead, the gifts still showered
on our lowered heads and be washed
by the Grace flowing all around us.

Where will we be then?

You are not homeless here.
Nor do you simply trudge
upon an unawakened object.
No illegals walk the Earth.
No aliens here, we are creatures
co-creating the World together.
At best, we conceive of her
as a mother, and so expect
the bounty of a mother's love
unending, unearned, unconditional.
At worst, She is an It, waiting
to be exploited for profit,
to ease ambitious appetites
of those who swallow
in big bites, without ever
tasting the rich sweetness.
Wake up, become aware!
Our waiting world is
needing care, alive and willing
to share her healing and her bounty.
But Earth is finite, though
infinitely patient with our
reckless profligration,
and to survive might
have to shrug us off.
And where will we be then?

Come listen to the Garden

Why do birds sing?
Is it to tell their flock
about the hawk that
hunts on higher winds?
Is it a way to say all clear,
all clear, it's safe to gather
here, come feast, come eat
its safe, tweet, tweet, all clear.
Come here, come hear our song.
Does Life itself need to declare
its presence here, flittering in the
green, this vibrant living scene?
What might they say
about the way we squawk
and define our territory?
Why the war of words, and
why we seek to dominate
and shriek above all else
because we fear to share the air.
Can song be valued if
its not heard? Is it absurd
to believe the worth of
words that are not heard?
These thoughts distract from the fact
its pleasant in the garden; and the Joy
I feel deep in my core that you
have taken time today to read the words
I've used to say how blessed we are by life.

Cosmic Energy

Last night the moon was dark
and tonight eclipsed
the layering of shadows,
might that explain
the edginess we felt
sitting still within the circle?
We gathered as we always do,
and settled in the silence
yet distraction beckoned
us away from our
practiced tranquility.
How then must it be
outside amongst the revelry
created by those who use
cosmic energy to excuse
abuse of themselves and others?
I pray that the peace we seek
will be extended to all we meet
out on the street.
And through our practice
we might see the love
that is always there for
us, and all others needing care.

Fear of Flying

Its hard to trust
in things unseen
when life's been
rough, and good
choices lean. So
trying to control
it all may seem a
reasonable alternative.
Except as you hold
the reigns in tighter
grip, the possibilities

begin to slip faster
through your fingers.
Until one day,
if you are blessed,
you come to see
your life's a mess
and realize it's due,
in part, to you trying
to analyze the depths
before you put a toe in.
If that day comes,

and I hope it will,
it may be like
charging toward a cliff,
release the brake, and take
a breath down into your belly,
all the world is waiting
with baited hope,
to lift you up, right at the edge,
and even as you fear the end
you will find yourself flying.

Remembering Mary

You came to me
in memory when
I was first woke
this morning.
Like a fragment
of a dream, the longing
for you lingered.
I forgot to lift
the small burdens
your legacy left me.
You triumphed over
more than most
will ever need to face,
but still some rocks
placed in your path have
tripped me up and
made me limp.
Anything you failed
to give, was missing
from your plate.
The feast you laid
and the bills you paid
were forged from
will and wit.
The love we shared,
the life we've dared
to birth from loss
and need, caused scars
I wear as emblems
like medals on a soldiers
chest, denoting bravery.
I awoke this morning,
and heard your voice again,
singing the blues softly.

Leave it to the Angels

Some days I feel like
an avenging angel
fiery sword drawn
ready to pierce
arrogant hearts
in order for loving
compassion to flow.
In fantasy I swoop
low and upend the
status quo, having read
the hearts of the hateful,
thereby sure where to
wield my sword.
Certain that each slice
would sever
the fear and loathing
projected on unwary
targets; the haters' hate
lays like bloated
corpses in the dregs
of life denied.
But then, thank God,
and all her saints,
I shake myself awake,
and grateful not to be
blinded by righteousness
I turn back to Love, and
leave it to the angels.

Your Parting

A thousand words have failed to say
how beauty pulses in love's blood
and pumps longing in the air that
Life breathes in big gulps. How is
peace possible when desire cuts
deeper, deeper ruts in anguished heart?
And in still moment between breath
beats awareness of loneliness
for I am left behind, even as you've taken
parts of me away, and every day
your missing presence surrounds me.
Still here and gone, I hold on
to memories of tiny things, the tune
you hummed, the music of your tapping
feet as you walked away that morning.
How many times, as you retreat,
have I chased you up that street,
within my mind, to entreat
and beg you to stay a while longer.
And if you had, would you still live,
and who would I be then?
For your parting and my grief
have opened paths for me to take
and etched designs into my dreams
that helped me love again.

Don't hate the haters.

Don't hate the haters;
though they deserve
no less, perhaps, for
riot of pain they cause.
Those fear fucked fools,
who try to sow shame
and loathing, and use it
for the power it brings.
Not because it will please God.
God is not amused.
Fight, resist, speak out
but do not invite hate
in nor foster it in others.
You will be leasing room
in your heart to the enemy,
just handing the keys to
abusers who will spit on
your soul and wipe their
dirty boots on your dreams.
Do not hate the haters, Live.
Live Big. Love. And smile
at their confusion as you
blossom and they die on the vine.

Self Talk

A soft chime in the distance
echoes vibrant longing
in closed throat, dust dry
from lack of use.
Life is here within.
choke off the sibilant
hiss inside who denies
you space to be open
to your verdant clarity.
Love, like water, relentlessly
carves caverns, reshapes inner landscapes.
Open the floodgates, a simple "yes" will do.

The Final Frontier

Do you feel empty inside?
Hit the pause button, and
breath into the vastness.
You will not be lost, not
swallowed up by need.
Take a moment to heed
your way in the darkness;
attention makes it
holy. You are not lost
or broken. You've been
awakened, a chance
is blossoming in the
vacuum. Greet the fear
that demands distraction.
Don't eat to bursting.
Don't drink to delirium.
Don't pull the vapors
of forgetfulness into
your verdant lungs.
Welcome escape from
oblivion is waiting for
you—don't hurry by.
Rest for a moment
it may not feel safe,
we've been conditioned
to believe we are not enough.
Wait, see the stars? You are.
You are safe among the stars
whose dust is in you.
There is a galaxy of space inside
And love's the only occupant.

Where you live

What if you lived
in a world that
also lived in a
universe that also
lived in a multiverse
Alive, Aware, Loving.
You do. And even
the aphid farmed
by the ant is known
and nurtured. You are
vital in the dance,
as is every Other.
Love, add love, be kind.
You matter more
than you know.
Sow your mind,
bring compassion.
All is waiting in
Welcome, Come.

Past Perception

Can I look and really see
behind the object
in front of me?
There is a deeper reality
hiding in the open.
Right there, or here,
waiting to be viewed
with dignity imbued.
Yet it's best seen
by softening the eyes;
for a hardened focus
only observes blurred motion.
Spirit informs all there is
and Love creates the Spirit.
We and the view are one.
How much effort do we invest
trying to look our best,
we who by our very vision
create the world we all live in.
How can we be so invested
in claiming our passivity
as just another chunk of content?
Creator Creating Creatures
And vice versa.

No Regrets

When I was small,
I would have done what I could
to have you let me stay,
and for you to say you loved me.
I'd have turned myself in two,
or painted myself blue, or tried to
meet all the needs of others.
When I was small I'd have tried
to stay that way, and not be in the way
if it meant I could stay with the family.
Though now I'm grown I still play
according to rules I made, out of what
I thought was said, by those I thought
should love me, and now are dead.
And still I try to fill the needs
of passersby, in search
of love and a place for me
to be within community.
And yet there are other reasons, too
for me to focus care on you, for I have
learned to read each need so clearly.
And I have learned that we are one
and the loving just begun
to blossom when we grow in peace together.
I know the love that once I sought outside,
resides in everything and everyone
and ought not be wasted on regrets.

Bone of Contention

Is there some law, like gravity,
that creates the urge to see
each challenge to our belief,
as a threat to our existence?
With never a thought of retreat,
or even agree to meet for coffee
where we might find some
common grounds,
so certain that we're right
we fight fire with fire.
I'll see your ire, and raise it.
Perhaps I'm old and too tired
to treat each threat you mete
upon me as inspired.
And God knows, that I am
"spoiled" by living here on
free soil where my woman's
voice is at least allowed to be
heard on the streets, without
threat of violent reprisal.
When you try to shut me up,
you remind me of a pup,
nipping at the heels of its mother.
So certain it has a right,
and never anticipating the bite
left in the old bitch.
It never ceases to amaze
how some never pass the phase
of entitlement, so confident
in their own correctness,
that for the sake of Love,
they hate.

Quantum Healing

I am swimming in a field
of possibilities. Unseen
currents handed down
through generations
move me in ways
and at speeds
not of my
making.
How
can
I
be
free
to be
me when
I can't see
the patterns
working in life
surrounding all of us?
What beliefs can I hold
that are sufficiently bold
to counter those that impose
limits on my impetuous creativity?
Good Luck and Miracles come to mind
when pondering the powers of humankind
to generate healing for all who share this tired planet.

Out

I want to come out
out of the quiet closet
out as the loud-mouthed
fat juicy-hearted floozy
that I am.
I want to come out
out of the cautious quiet
hushed toned propriety
that sucks the soul's marrow
from spontaneous bones.
I want to come out
outloud and lively,
I want to stomp and clump;
dancing in my shitkickers.
Ouch! Did I trod your toes?
I want to come out
out with my big bawdy laugh
that rattles the windows
where prune faces peak
and judge behind soiled lace.
I want to love you, or
hate you, right to your face.
I want to live out now
before I am dust
kicked around the fires
by the infamous
with long memories.
And if they judge me,
let them laugh outloud
and nod their heads
as if in agreement.

Hatt Kelley

Conformity

When I was young and full of pip
my parents loved and nurtured me
to the best of their ability.
Sometimes it was hard for them to see
me for who I was, and not a reflection
of parts of them that'd faced rejection.
And when they failed in that task
their spirits railed against
the thought of my going out
amongst society, unmasked.
For me to risk being seen as me
reminded them of times they tried
to be, and failed miserably.
Or worse when they stood bravely
and with a portion of pride,
only to be denied by those
who loved and feared for them.
And so the pattern goes on and on
a desire to be, fights with fear,
and a need for safety.
Yet still authenticity calls
in a voice quiet and strong
and every time we conform
from fear, we feel that
we've been wronged.
And so we carry on
passing the repression
like salt at the family table.

The Sacrifice

It's ancient
the story told of
sacrifice for others.
The inevitable death
that defies the lies
told by the powerful
who tries to contain
or restrain what they
can not comprehend.
Then the mystery in
which we see victory
over fear and tyranny
and even over death itself.
So rich the imagery,
the awe filled vulnerability,
its easy to be overwhelmed
by the end of story.
When the stone is rolled away
and the women come to mourn
find the grave is filled with light,
God in human form made right
the sins and suffering for all
and having finished the task
is unmasked as Messiah.
At what point in the story
does your spirit give
it's little leap of faith?
It is easy to be caught
by the martyr, and not
the unearned gift
of grace and love.

The Ritual

Darkened church, cold cave
death accepted and then denied.
The light returns to the earth
that gave us birth and sustains us
The fire's lit and passed,
a small flame multiplied,
raised high in hands above crowd
who's gathered to pay respect
to the turning back from death to life.
Alleluias sound, as bells sing,
flame kissed water brings
new life sprinkled on bowed heads.
The sacrifice has been made,
the world again is once saved.
Turn from suffering, and be eased,
light and life has triumphed.
Believe and rejoice.

The Calling

Sometimes joy pierces
my defenses, cutting
through self pity, and
obsession with paltry
things like possessions,
material or otherwise.
My body reacts with
tears and at times
songs burst forth.
There's nothing quiet
peaceful or calm;
not pleasant or nice,
my joy is a fire
consuming all ire.
Thankfully it passes
quickly for it is hard
to look humble when
God comes to call.

My love

You are a gentle rain
in a drought-ravaged night.
The memory of your face
shakes loose sad thoughts
from my heart mind,
like a fall wind rattles
the last leaves from bare trees.
In the winter of my life
I will live in spring
because I know you, and
no matter how we turn out,
it is enough to remember
that once we were together
shrouded by the summer fog
and love.

What's the Cost?

Have you ever seen
a person achieve
their dream in a single
moment?
The years of work
that went in, don't show,
just the whole world
aglow in fulfillment.
And your eyes and
heart fill and you
can't turn away from
the thrill of another
person's joy.
It is easy then to know
we are one, and
all success shines,
here in the moment.
Why compete for
the mythical peak
when we complete
the picture so neatly
by being together?
Could sharing be
the healing balm
our ancient star requires?
Shall we embrace a
moment's grace and
let the striving fade away
except when shared
among the many?

New old Friends

Old friend in new body!
My heart leaps to greet
you again, again, again.
Help me to remember who
I am. The I am that I am
in the time between times.
I will hold the mirror for you.
Hear the love; constant
containment internal space;
the cosmic dance. See!
We are here again, again.
Clasp my hand, we will heal
while we're here in body
and songs will swell in heaven.
The light that we return to
will flare brighter for our Joy
in meeting again, again, old friend.

Diversity

Your quirkiness helps me
create the space to simply be.
By being you, both dark
and light, especially
the prickly bits; I am encouraged.
We matter here, you and I,
as much as those who never
doubt the fact that they belong,
who never fear they're wrong,
and feel completely justified
in all they do.
We may feel uninvited and on
the outside looking in, but begin
to look within and you'll see
the truth. The earth is dust
without us loving others
just as they are. And if we fail
to even try because we buy
the tale that doesn't even see us,
the whole world will descend
into a lifeless trend where colors
blend to gray, and Joy will fade away.
So be the freak you're meant to be
and wave your flag bravely and
look around and you will see
some of us are dancing gleefully.

The Current Copy

Trying to trust which parts
of me must be released,
so my joy and productivity
can expedientially increase
can be very tricky.
Perhaps its not up to me
to decide which parts to delete,
to hide, and which to let ride.
But who else would be sufficiently clear
on which pieces I hold dear,
and which are window dressing?
Maybe if instead of looking at the content,
I examine the way it came to be
I will see what's wanting to be set free,
so I can travel lighter, faster,
and with more integrity.

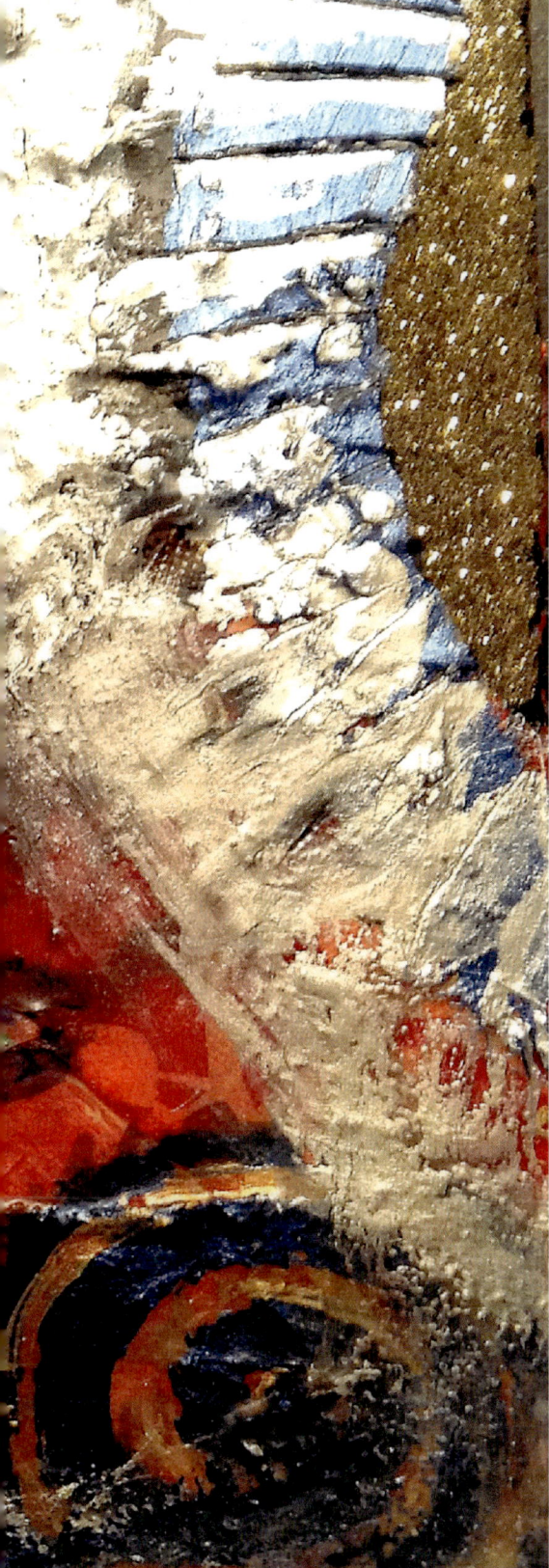

Life's Lessons

When learning something new
be ready for each step you do
to feel as though
it's lit up by a spot light
for all the world to view.
So every step must be right
(remember its taken in plain sight)
and you tend to review (again, again!)
the goal in mind before
any action's taken.
So it goes for quite a while,
every step is full of guile
and each struggle
watched by humankind!
You can't return to innocence
for now you know what
you don't know; there is
no turning back, but persevere,
and you will see an easing
in your mind, the steps
become second nature,
you've learned the thing, its done.
And all is peaceful once again,
until a new lesson is begun.

Night Blessing

Rest your head
here, softly lay
it down. The day
is done and gone.
Dreams sweetly
call, come, let go
of any woe
that blossoms
in your heart.
Tomorrow will
wait for you
to begin anew.
Breath deeply
·let sleep ease
your being.
All is well.
Be Peace.

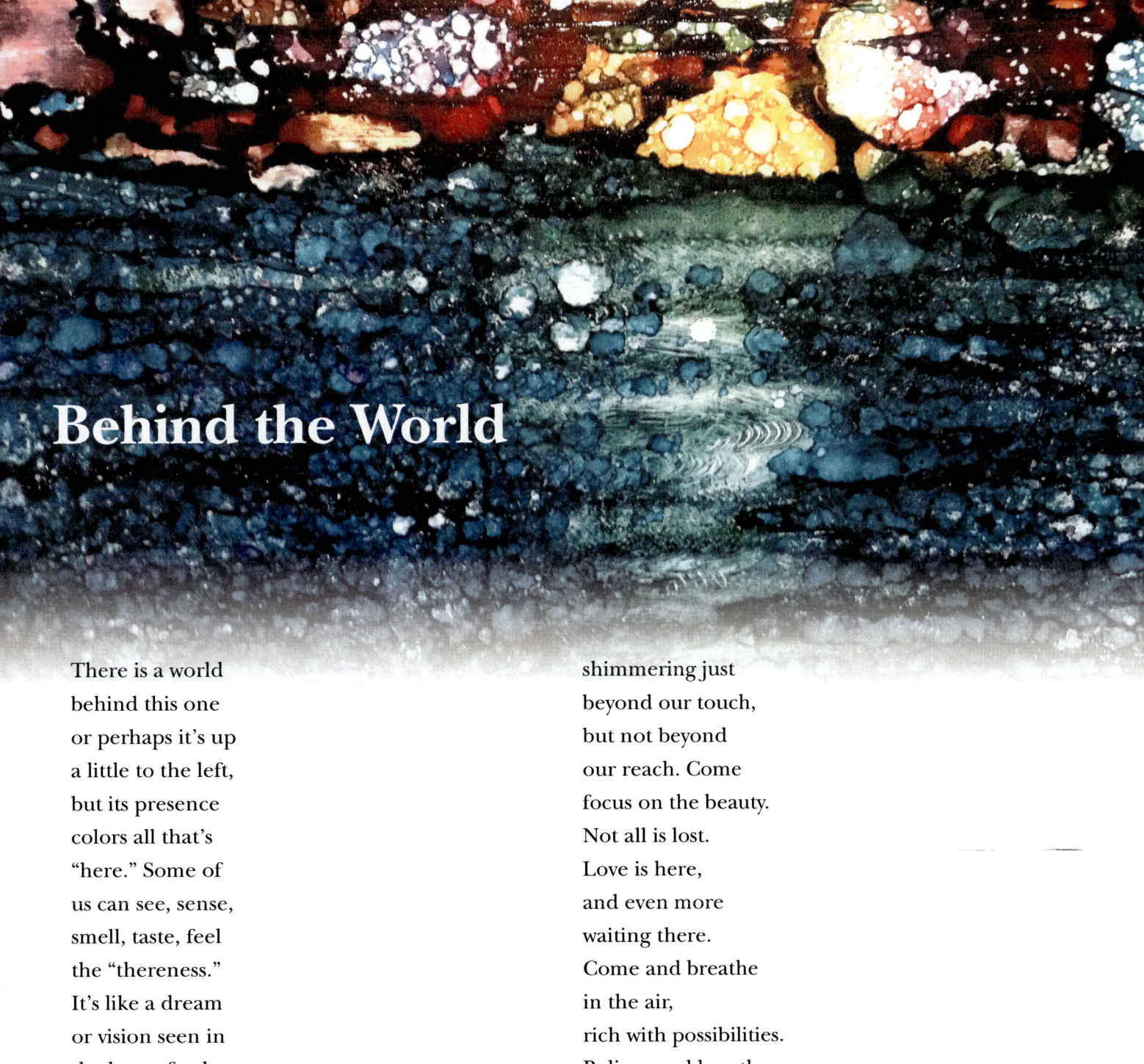

Behind the World

There is a world
behind this one
or perhaps it's up
a little to the left,
but its presence
colors all that's
"here." Some of
us can see, sense,
smell, taste, feel
the "thereness."
It's like a dream
or vision seen in
the heat of a desert,
shimmering just
beyond our touch,
but not beyond
our reach. Come
focus on the beauty.
Not all is lost.
Love is here,
and even more
waiting there.
Come and breathe
in the air,
rich with possibilities.
Believe and breathe.

Choosing Peace

What's the difference how you act,
when you're challenged or attacked,
isn't any response used to defend
justified in the end?
I've been safe most of my life.
I've not been bombarded with strife,
but I have seen enough to know
that frontal assault has got to go,
even when it is purely defensive.
In my experience it doesn't work,
you end feeling like a jerk,
and everything escalates until
alternative choices are nil.
How then can we react in a way
that may support greater calm?
Is it possible to take a breath
before we decide to take
a stand we can't get out of?
Can we choose to respond
with kindness, rather than in kind,
and in doing so spare us all
from feeling in a bind
and fighting to be rescued?
I'll choose kindness when I can
and try to teach it, too,
and hope one day
that I can choose peace
over entering the fray.

When loss comes,
and its complete
with no hopes of
retreat, it must be
honored. Though
every fiber of your
being demands denial
and feels like fleeing
from the pain, stop
and acknowledge
the beauty and power
of what is gone. Take
as long as you can for
the depth of your grief
will someday determine
the relief you feel for
having mourned well.
And through the process
you will find that love
remains behind and
when you come out
from the daze, you'll
be amazed that what
was lost is found
but in a way that's
changed. For love
transcends when
it is finally freed
and only then can it
begin to ease the world
of suffering within.
The suffering within.

The
Grief
Process

When will the flow stop?

Will the words dwindle
down slowly until they drop
like a splat of water from
a leaky pipe, or a tear
from a red-rimmed eye?
Fear comes up even as
I think of stemming
creative flow. For me
it's speaking not thinking
that confirms I am. All
is relational. You
and I, me with me, i am
and the supreme "I am."
I can speak without words
but they are so handy,
for my arms cannot hug
the world. I cannot lay
my head on each shoulder
to seek and offer comfort.
If when the end, or pause
begins, I trust the silence
will contain love enough
to sustain hope for me
to go on, and grace to be
the receiver as well as the gift.

Beauty Full

I see you as I see myself
beautiful because I show up
again, again. Perhaps you
don't understand I stand up
and offer love risking all.
I see you as you see me too.
Did I speak my truth today?
Without rancor I said how
I needed you and hoped
you'd hear me offering
myself up like a chalice.
Here, sip my sweetness,
know how you taste
on my lips, and let freedom
role on your tongue like honey
as you swallow my meaning.
Here is my heart wear it lightly.
We are wholly right and
way left of center and my words
can't hurt, only heal what was
already broken and needing hope.
Please allow me to sigh and breathe.
You are so beautiful.

Winter Solstice (for Tim)

It is easier in comparison,
to go forth with sword in hand
slicing through all
that denies you of the prize.
Though the ground's uneven;
some players born far down the field,
still how much easier to strive and stride
through life with salvaged pride,
failing perhaps, but with head held high.

What value has the waiting game?
To remain open to prevailing winds
and whatever they blow in;
to set intention and
receive in its own good time.
To sit with open hands
resting in the longing,
closed eyes still searching
for impending Grace.
The candle lit to brave the dark
and blaze a way for all who wander,
yes, that is a good that's praised.
But who dares to sit within dark days
listening closely for the slow return of light?

Lambs and Goats

How'd you come to be
the sacrificial lamb?
Was the honor handed
down within your family?
Was it you who tried to save
the others of your group
by being seen as the one
who craved destruction?
There's many of us
in the world though we
are told there's not.
We walk with lowered heads
our Spirits curled in knots.
We stagger from the poison
that we imbibe ourselves
for it preserves our place,
and even though we're outcasts,
we still serve the human race
as scapegoats.

Fall from Grace

Do I seem bitter?
Perhaps it would be
better if I closed
my eyes and never
said all the sadness
in my head and heart.
But I've been gathered in
by others who are gone,
and they have shared
how much they cared
for all of us still here.
I have known
some tragedy in
the life I've lived and
feel compelled to
share the gift of
lessons garnered there.
Though I try to speak
for those who can't
do I betray the goal
I've tried to reach?
It's a slippery slope and
not for me to preach
a life I cannot live;
one filled with hope.
I've seen suffering,
and I've known it too,
but underneath it all
Beauty exists and
Grace has always
stopped my fall.

No miracle to write home about

Do you have one?
A searing second that swamps
your memory banks and
floods your heart?
It plays in the mind
like the end of a film
flickering before the lights
come up. Some triggered
thought, a sound, some
scent brings him back to me
the moment he had to leave.
There was no choice but for me
to stay. He had to go
though I remained
assured thank God, of our love.
Left my body too, but was
snatched back at the edge

by the silver cord that
snapped to set him free
from pain and misery.
He had no choice, no offer
to leave the light behind,
no miracle to write home about.
How heaven is aligned
right next to the living, a half a step
away. Some would call it
a trauma, I've often in the past,
but now I see the wisdom
in slipping free so easily.
I know I'll be greeted
when I let fall the robe and
step into shining brightness
of the next room over. I will
be gathered in again and we
will embrace the plan, well laid
and played, that made me
who I am.

Come the Revolution (Nubbins Unite)

To grow up in a place
is to take a space in line.
The group starts to define
your role and who you
were is left behind.
Or you may stay
deep down inside
where it's possible to hide
under all the social trappings.
Pinned and piled they abide
on your outsides until the weight
no longer can be denied and
you're ground down to a nubbin.
A nubbin you remain until
one day you face the pain
of shedding all the dross;
and you strain to recreate
the you who once was lost.
And there you stand for all to see,
bathed in vulnerability and suddenly
being hidden doesn't seem so bad.
Give yourself time my friend,
and pretend that all is as it should be;
there may be other nubbins
watching furtively, and you
the fondest hope of many.
And someday we may all rise,
nubbins united, and the balance
may be righted as we raise our
weary heads and ease
our work worn backs to seek
the prize previously denied
by those who wrote the rules.

Oh Bright Girl!

Oh Bright Girl!
Like sun on water
you sparkle, a reflection
of the larger Mystery.
The world awaits you
and longs to swing
you in its arms in dizzy
circles of delight. Do not
cast your sweet innocence
away as if it has no value.
But neither guard it
at all cost. You are
of infinite Beauty, and as
you live, your heart
will be battered and
broken open, that is as
it should be, for a treasure
must be discovered before
it can be shared. And in the
giving, it grows deeper and
strengthens until one day
in the far away; all that is
left is Love.

God(dess)

Our voices are calling.
Siren song drawing
beckoning embrace
Come! Lay your head
and heart safely here.
Sisters shine a beacon.
Gleeful giggles or
solemn sighs are
welcome, welcome
Stomp inside the
moist cave, juicy myth
drum your feet
awaken Mother
let her sing out
from our hands
from our eyes
from our baying throats,
our heads thrown back
and mouths open to the stars.
Have we lured you to the rocks?
So be it. It was never about you.

Among the Missing

When I was a kid,
before I had letters
I was absorbed
by far away pictures
in the geographic rag.
They called to me,
"This is your world.
We are waiting."
Then one day
a list was printed
of animals soon
to be missing.
Gonegonegone
from our world, forever.
Curiously, at the same time
faces like mine began
to appear on milk
cartons saying, "Missing."
In my mind, the kids
and the creatures
were together playing,
somewhere outside,
rough and tumble.
And I was stuck
at the family table
trying to avoid drinking the juice
that tasted like poison to me.
I fantasize still that
soon the local sacred hill
will crack open and all
the missing will walk
backbackback
into our world.
Giggling and roaring
their untamed delight
in having hidden for so long.

Soften

Soften your eyes
come realize
your heart and
mine are one.
Soften your gaze,
you'll be amazed.
Love rings a bell.
There is no hell,
except of our own making.
Soften your heart
its only smart
you are a part
of all there is.
Open yourself
The longer you wait
the stronger the hate
lay down the weight
that burdens your heart.

Soften your thoughts.
Let go of the pain
of battles you fought
and lost; the bitterness
gained only poisons you.
Let yourself grieve
we will wait here
care cupped in our hands.
for when you are ready.
Soften to Life.
It isn't just strife
There is grace
And beauty here.
Just Soften your eyes
come realize
your heart and
mine are one.
Love rings a bell.

About the Author

Harriett "Hatt" Kelley is a hairdresser-turned-chaplain, artist, author and energy minister. She specializes in helping others use spiritual practices to promote understanding healing, growth, and joy. Hatt lives in San Francisco with her husband of 30+ years, Tim.

A message from Hatt:
Please connect with me on Facebook at Hatt Kelley's Creative Conspiracy.
My original artwork is available for purchase at hattkelley.com.

44878489R00069

Made in the USA
Middletown, DE
18 June 2017